ACCLAIM FO

"I've known Mitra for some years.... ...ing heart have nudged me again and again towards the light at the exact moments when I most needed guidance, protection and healing. Now at last, for those who have not yet had the opportunity to benefit from Mitra's unique gifts and skills, his book INSIGHTS offers a series of teachings and life lessons, drawn from profound experience and accessible to all. The statements he offers are lean -- no wasted fat in this excellent writing! -- and every word hits home with thought-provoking impact."

—Graham Hancock,
bestselling author of *Fingerprints of the Gods*,
and *America Before: The Key to Earth's Lost Civilizations*

"Mitra is a gifted healer who has been inspired by real life events. In this book, he shares his empowering, inspirational gift of poetry, giving the reader keys to transformation, healing and contentment."

—Anita Moorjani,
New York Times best-selling author of
*Dying To Be M*e and *What if This Is Heaven*

"An insight is an event that happens in our consciousness that changes us forever. Mitra, a gifted healer, not only facilitates insights in others but continues to be available to his own inner revelations as well. This book is evidence of both. They are recorded insights that shifted him put in a form that will shift others, including you. Now dive in and be transformed again and again."

—Michael B. Beckwith,
Founder & Spiritual Director, Agape International Spiritual
Center, Author, *Life Visioning* and *Spiritual Liberation*

"*Insights* is just that—a collection of Mitra's deep insights that, when you take a few moments to contemplate them and meditate on them, will lead you back into the awareness, acceptance and expression of the pure sacred essence of who you are."

—Jack Canfield,
Coauthor of the #1 New York Times bestselling
Chicken Soup for the Soul® series and *The Success Principles*™

"The quiet calm of Mitra's hard-won understanding is emanating from *Insights: Steps to Truth*. I read the words and feel the resonance not just of his wisdom, but what it feels like to remember *Home*, and my eternal place within its vast embrace. In this beautiful book, Mitra gives us insights to help us navigate through the muddy waters of persistent illusions and incomplete understandings. His words remind us of the inevitable opportunity at the heart of every challenge, about the excruciating bliss of true surrender. I use Mitra's *Insights* every day to live, and I am certain I will use these poignant reminders when it comes my time to die."

—Kimberly Carter Gamble,
Producer, Director and Writer:
THRIVE II: This is What it Takes

"I have had the blessing of knowing Mitra as a friend, a mentor and a beacon of the humility and warmth of a true source of loving wisdom. With this book he has quietly offered up an authentic map and effective user manual for the inner and interpersonal challenges of real-life. At first blush INSIGHTS: Steps to Truth my seem like just a beautiful little book of simple poetry - and it is. It's also so much more than that. These hard-won realizations are a guide for truly healing and nurturing the soul, and provide a compass toward an authentic, compassionate and creative life."

—Foster Gamble, Co-creator,
THRIVE Movie and *THRIVE Movement*

INSIGHTS

STEPS TO TRUTH

MITRA POLITI

ISBN 978-9968-49-506-6

Cover Design and Interior Typesetting by Richell Balansag

With great love and respect
this book is dedicated to PachaMama
Community

CONTENTS

FOREWORD

M itra delivers the reader an entry point into stillness. His words capture the essence of silence and guide all who are drawn to his work into the experience of the profound truth that lives within them.

I am honored to be able to call him both a mentor and friend.

In Insights his transparency and vulnerability guides you from the pain of separation and duality into the profound experience of love and oneness.

His years of devotion and dedication are a gift to all who are ready to experience the truth of themselves.

Access the breakthroughs that await you now and be forever transformed.

Peace & Blessings,

- Panache Desai
International best-selling author of *Discovering your Soul Signature* and *You are Enough*

INTRODUCTION

How this book was born

This story began writing itself at a moment of significant change in my life. It was a moment in time in which reality took a turn, a turn I could never have prepared for or anticipated.

This moment arrived after a period of many years of intense, inner work. I had been living a life of dedicated spiritual practice that included meditation, countless silent retreats, living and working side-by-side with a spiritual teacher and working as a practitioner of alternative medicine. In those days I participated in and facilitated self-development and personal transformation workshops, working with hundreds of participants over the years.

My personal understanding and experience of a spiritual life and practice had been deeply established. I had lived many experiences of expanded consciousness, existential love and encounters with the inner silence of my being.

It was during this period that I met who I thought was the love of my life. It was a deep meeting on the soul level, and a profound experience of universal love. My devotion to this relationship gave birth to a level of love I had never known existed. I was able to bring the expression of my spiritual world into my relationship and married life. The sweetness of this meeting between my connection to Spirit and the love for a human being merged into one and blossomed into 8 years of partnership and marriage.

During this time we were living in an spiritual community; a community that provided a rich quality of life and deep friendships amongst its members. Because we were going through a powerful and intimate growth process which demanded great sacrifice, the bond between community members was unique and special.

My partner and I established our lives, built our home and ran personal development workshops together. After 6 1/2 years of partnership, we decided to bring a child into this world. We had a beautiful baby girl. I felt as if I was reaching new levels of growth in the experience of family life and deepening my roots.

This was the moment when my life turned upside down. With no forewarning, my partner came to me and told me that our relationship was over. Both my inner and outer worlds came crumbling down and my reality shattered into pieces. Not only was marriage falling apart but I was also a young father to a one-year-old child.

It took eight months after our separation for the truth to come out: my partner had been having a secret affair with a friend and fellow community member.

During this time period, I lived with constant lies and manipulations that affected not only my personal and family life but also created divisions within our inner circle of friends and community. Everything I had ever known was undermined.

In the harsh reality of our separation, and as a young father with little experience, I was filled with confusion and despair. I no longer had confidence that I could discern what was true and what was a lie, what was right and what was wrong.

As a way to strengthen myself, I decided to sit down and write that which would reflect and invoke the power of Creation which had always been my guide.

I wrote to remind myself of the realizations that I had harnessed as a result of my inner work and spiritual inquiry; I wrote to have a tool to return to truth. This is how this book you are holding was born.

In retrospect, I can see that this dark night of the soul was part of a process of deeper evolution on my path. It tested me in every spiritual understanding that I had gathered up until this point and forced me to reach deeply into the only thing that could carry me through - faith. Faith in life, creation and myself. I discovered new ways of to heal myself and ultimately I was opened to a new level of embodiment in what I could share in a healing and teaching context with others.

Although I did not know it at the time, I can see now that life had a bigger plan for me and that this crisis was something

I needed to pass through in order evolve and give birth to a more refined and precise offering. Now, with the passage of time, I can say that the experience was a blessing in disguise.

How to use this book

In the beginning I wrote simply for myself, to gain insight, inspiration and strength. Sometimes the words seemed to write themselves, as if coming from a source of spiritual guidance beyond myself. Sometimes I drew from the wisdom I had gained in my own personal journey.

In the process of reading these words to myself, the words empowered and guided me. I was reconnected to a Higher Source and a deep truth that was already in me.

I invite you to investigate within yourself the influence of these words. Read each verse with presence and allow yourself time to feel and absorb the meaning contained within the words. My wish is that any person that reads these words may also be strengthened in the face of struggle, and guided home to Truth.

LIFE

L ife is full of

Wonder

Beauty

And Love

This is a fact…

Acknowledge this fact to the depths of your heart
And to the core of your being

❦

Life is not an endless party
It is the infinite celebrating itself

❦

A journey of human life
Is a journey of friction

Between darkness and light
Love and fear
Pain and freedom
Between memory and forgetfulness

On this journey of life
Change is the only constant
The light is ever present, guiding it all
Leading me from confusion into clarity
And from doubt into certainty
The morning comes
Bringing the hope of a new dawn

You, who did not forsake me
You, who shines in my heart
And lights my path
Who has answered my prayers

It is You I see within me
My beacon of light through the darkness
It is to You that I give thanks

TRUTHFULNESS

There is no correct answer that comes
from the thinking mind
The mind which dissects into small pieces
The truth comes from the belly
From a deeper, more basic place

Take care of yourself by listening to your gut feelings
In this way you will be connected to what is real
Your authentic truth

When we allow ourselves to be naked
We can be seen for who we really are
We are all human

We have forgotten how to be exposed
Not only to the truth
But how to be naked in front of ourselves
We are developing a pattern of
rejecting our own humanity
And so we cover it in evermore layers

Success does not come from conquering the outer world
Success comes from self fulfillment
The naked truth will be revealed
When you can be naked
Naked with truth itself

Coming back to myself
Through expression and creativity
Without being dependent on the other

Coming back to myself
By the truth which is born from within
The truth which is already in me

Words of truth lead to truth
Lies disguise the Divine
Hiding the beauty of the infinite

Being in denial
Creates a painful illusion
To create illusion
Is to create a false hope

An intention to be in integrity
Or an attempt to conceal
At the root of the intention for integrity, lies the truth
At the root of the attempt to conceal, lies self deception

In seeing things for what they truly are
In confronting the illusion and the lie
Arises a subtle resistance
This resistance must be melted by compassion
Compassion for myself
Compassion for the other

That which I have seen
I cannot reveal
That which I have experienced
I cannot pass on
That which I am
I can only be

I undress in front of myself
I feel free in the face of my pain
I feel free with the Divine in me
With my own humanity

In this way, I can see what is happening in my world
In this way, I will be able to testify to the change
To the mystery which guides me
Only from a state of truth can I point out the truth

CHANGE

In every extreme shift of circumstances
In the movement away from stability
Once there
Now gone
We live a process of deep inner change

The perception of who we are
What this world around us is
And how we see the people of this world
Must necessarily change

It is a time when, whether we like it or not
Our perception of reality transforms
Either we develop a deeper anxiety towards life
Or we mature into a more complete understanding

Such times in our lives
Will always be critical points in our development
And mark the crossroads
Towards positive evolution or bitterness

No real change can come from willpower alone
Willpower must be accompanied by true inspiration
The inspiration born of a renewed connection
With the inner self that IS
Beyond time and space
Inspiration that springs from freedom itself
And discovers the freedom within

Times of transition bring changes
To all facets of being and experience

We cannot preserve the past
For the new is knocking at the door

Let go of the old
So that the new can be received

Combine strength with truth and inspiration
And give birth to manifestation

The question to ask ourselves is:

**Are we opening up to Creation,
Or are we hiding in limitation?**

A new consciousness is birthing
While the old one is not yet dead
Aim for that new consciousness within you
And it will lead you to new horizons
Clean and fresh dimensions of being

DESIRE

Clinging to desire creates separation
Letting go of desire brings unity
Between oneself and the Divine
Between oneself and Creation

In each desire resides a layer of tension
This tension is a current of frustration and fear
Intermingled with excitement
For the new and unknown

Understand the nature of desire
And frustration will disappear
Free yourself to the new and fear will subside
Surrender into the unknown
The sacred will reveal itself

THE EGO

A momentary illusion of success
And already the ego tries to claim it
A momentary feeling of failure
And already the ego redefines itself
Whether to build itself up or diminish itself
It aims always to be in the center

Act from the mind
And you will become a politician -
One who changes his religion and point of view
According to opinions of the masses
And the whims of the other

Meet all that you encounter on your path
Eye to eye and heart to heart

On this journey
I have met the world from above
I have met the world from below
But when I met the world
Eye to eye and heart to heart

I saw it

In wonder

For the very first time

PAIN

To Truth -
The Divine within me
I call out:
Reveal your light in me
Every moment more…

So that my pain will subside
Like water evaporating to the heights
To dissolve into Source

The pain hurts yet it also purifies and heals
It softens the sharp edges of the personal wound
The process is necessary
To change me
To soften me

Meet the truth within the pain
Not the lies of victimhood
Discover the treasures hidden within it

To seek assurance and solutions from the other
In moments of weakness
To seek hope and solid ground outside of oneself
Brings only temporary relief
It is a but a painkiller
To mask the pain that comes from a deeper place

Mitra Politi

When the wave of emotion arrives
Allow it to be
Bring it closer to you
Let it cleanse you in complete faith

When a wave of negative thought arrives
Full of judgment, worries and fear
Run, dance, breathe and return to the body
Lose control into the essence

A floating voice within me stirs up pain
Silence surfacing in me opens up space
What I give my attention to is my free choice
Yet it is challenging…

Every experience of pain will also pass
Do not fight it nor follow it
Rather flow through it
It will pass

In gratitude for the name of the Creator
I bow in reverence to His being
I rejoice in Her essence
Blessed is the One who creates all change

Give thanks for every change
Give thanks for all that is here and now

Allow yourself to grieve, my son
For all that has happened
Allow yourself to experience the pain
For it exists and must be met through the heart
It is through the heart that it will be cleansed and
healed

All has been taken from me
Yet there is no sadness
This is the power of true love
A love that leaves me exposed to life
And grasping for the source of my deepest being
A love that leaves me clean after a storm

This moment carries new possibilities

    Of Liberation

      Freshness

      And Innocence

EMOTIONS

In the meeting between strong
emotion and Creation
There is liberation, change and growth

⟨∞⟩

This is the state of an emotional wound:

It refuses all help, yet cries for it
It rejects all, yet doesn't want to be rejected
It does not love, yet yearns for love
It fears everything, yet does not want to be afraid

⟨∞⟩

When you attempt to control the uncontrollable
You enslave yourself to stress and anxiety
When you devote yourself to the unknown
You surrender to love and beauty
And open to the power of life

When fear grows stronger
When all seems closed
Do not break
Do not flee
Face this primal fear, rooted deeply within you
Stand your ground
Look it in the eyes

When fear arises
It is hard to see what is real and what is illusion
Where reality begins and where it ends
Recognize this, and relax into not knowing
And the fear of fear itself will disappear

THE WARRIOR

The warriors I have met along this journey
Are kings who rule their inner kingdom
Those who have walked through the fire
And come out stronger

So it begins, and so it continues
Submerge yourself in confusion and uncertainty
And contraction and fear quickly arise…

One is frozen

In movement and trust
Seeing from the reference point of love
The pain and fear can be released

Go through the challenges
Not as a victim
But as a warrior
Rather than running away from the challenge
Run towards it

Learn to fight for life
Learn to fight for the good in you
And the good that surrounds you
Do not fight from the space which creates war
But from a space of true courage
To stand on two feet and go forward
Towards your dreams

Mitra Politi

HOPE AND TRUST

The path to inner peace
Is found within me
The river to inner peace
Flows in self love

I give thanks to the Divine within me
Even though it has yet to be revealed
I open to a new dialogue with Spirit
Even though I have not been given an answer

Even if this spring lies buried deep within me
May it resurface and overflow once again

The regret and the memories
The pain and tranquility
The love and unity
The desire and the longing
The struggle and the letting go
All of it, a wind that passes me by
As infinite forms of the spirit of Creation
Thousands of fragments of emotions
Memories swirling and falling away

I remain as a tree with strong roots in the ground
Watching the leaves as they shiver
Enjoying the infinite poetry of the wind
Witness to the Spirit of life
In surrender to the power of the experience

Mitra Politi

Just when I thought that the truth
within me had vanished
Covered by uncertainty
I entered
There she stood in all her glory
Waiting for me to dive into her depths
To bathe in her pure waters
She asks for nothing
Yet her gravity is full with the fuel of the Infinite

Guard my soul for it is a child of light
fragile and soft and filled with understandings
And misunderstandings
Opening once more
To grace and trust

❦

PRAYER

P rayer is the true nature of space -
An inner friend

The Divine exists within you
Connect with it
You do not need mediators
There is no need for masters nor servants
Buddha said – Be a light unto yourself!

The prayer becomes a blessing for the one who prays
The request becomes a longing to open to Creation

Peace to all understandings
Peace to all prayers

I pray that God rekindles my will
All that remains to do, is to let go
To release myself
To continue towards my own horizon
To the place that Spirit directs me to
And pulls me towards

My potential

It is a world of possibilities
A world full of gifts
A new consciousness

In Divine will
This trust will strengthen
In Divine will
It will grow roots within me

VULNERABILITY

E motions come and go
It is their nature
They take away the illusions of ego
They leave the human exposed and fragile
To a sweet vulnerability
which opens one up

My pride wants to prove that I've succeeded
That I have overcome the barriers of pain
That I am tall
But there is no tall nor short
It is all one big endless plain
Deep recognition of this carries within it infinite humility
And the path to those spaces is open once again
Making me more accessible
More human

I am fragile
Yet the wind blowing in my face is familiar
It is the soft wind which comes from infinite space
It reminds me of the inner wind
Blowing towards a new awakening
Towards an endless sky

I thank you God for putting me in this place
I had so much expectation
For a spiritual awakening

I forgot my origin, my longing for a blue sky
For a forgotten earth filled with flowers
The earth within me sprouting seeds
That shall bear fruit

How to seek an answer?
How to reach the place where the solution is revealed?

The longing for what is real
For the Divine
Blows into the wind
To Spirit it shall return

*   *Mitra Politi*

The song of love has touched me through pain
And offered me this time for me to know my own self
A time to connect with the unknown that dwells in me

So I can feel my breath once again
So I can feel the Beloved

THE INNER CHILD

The pain of the wounded inner child
Brought with it disconnection from joy

In the innocence beyond the wound
The inner child
Knows how to flow with life
He is thirsty for adventure
He does not fear the world but wants to live it
She is fully alive and hungry for life
She makes **every moment**
A time of innovation and renewal

THE SPIRITUAL EGO

After peeling away the layers of identity
A moment arrives that reveals the eternal truth

He who has touched the Divine -
The stillness of the Infinite within
Must be alert
For it is here that the spiritual ego awaits him
Trying to sneak in
With its false story of superiority

She who has experienced the direct kiss of Creation
May become certain of her uniqueness
That she is more evolved than the other

The Spiritual ego
Is a false mask that conceals itself from itself
Yet it is felt by its surroundings

In this moment where Creation opens itself to you
In the first kiss from the Divine
Do not let the ego convince you of your superiority

Know that it is simply **the beginning of a relationship**
Between Creation and your innermost self
In your highest form

Do not lie to yourself
And you shall not be deceived

INNER DEATH

To reinvent myself between two forces:
One is desire for change and expansion
The other is fear of losing what has been

I am passing through a personal death
That leaves me empty
An emptiness which prepares me for the new
I drop identities and die into it

I am free and have always been so...

⌘

RELEASING

B oth the free bird and the caged one
Exist in the same world

Remember to see things from the eyes of the free bird
From above
So you can perceive the bigger picture

To carry oneself caught between inner obstacles
Means a life of suffering
Trapped between the sensation of denial
And the effort to hold the pain at bay

To cross through these obstacles
Is to be fully present with the pain
So that the gates of the beyond can open
Into the inner space which is free of suffering
A space that knows how to enjoy vastness and freedom

A thought passes –
I have no strength of heart right now…

This is an opportune moment:
Since there is no strength left for a struggle with pain
The mind is now too weak to resist
It can only surrender and break free
After the contraction comes release

Keep on releasing - my dear son

Moments of anxiety lead to fear of life

Moments of fear lead to doubt

Moments of control lead to contraction

Moments of love lead to beauty

Moments of calm lead to release

Moments of harmony give birth to love

Mitra Politi

HEALING

R each deep within yourself
Without fear
Feel your heart with effortlessness
For it is only by the touch of love
That deep wounds can be healed
Not by falling into numbness
But in awakening

In times of emotional struggle
We tend to lose our ability to love ourselves

This disconnection comes
As a result of avoiding the experience of pain
At the same time it awakens within us
The longing that aims for self love

**The emotional immune system awakens
And wounds can heal**

When I heal the other, I heal myself
When I bless the other, I bless myself
May I bless all the goodness that comes my way…

The joy

     The aliveness

          The peace

     The success

The love

Bless the Oneness revealed in happiness

Open yourself and allow things to be as they are
Without trying to control them
Without wanting them to be different
Flowing with what is
With all that exists
So that heaviness will turn into great liberation

I am once again the master of the self
The master of my inner reality

Rebelling against the light of love
Is to resist your own self –
Though it brings a momentary and addictive satisfaction
It will chain you to the cycle of negativity

To walk and to be led by the light
Guided by love
Brings satisfaction and long lasting contentment
It will lead you to a cycle of goodness and beauty

In a chapter of life that seems to never end
Things come together in their own rhythm
There is a unique timing for healing

Divine timing
Which softens the stone of grief
The Holy Spirit
The essence of silence
That provides for all

Even to that which is forever clinging
Even to that which is forever contracted

Even when I cannot open up and trust
It is there to kiss my cheek

Send love to all
Send it to the enemy as well as to the beloved
Send it to a stranger
Send love to he who comes towards you
And to she who grows distant
In doing so, **the love within you will have a voice**

Send this love especially to your own self
To the deep unknown within you

SURRENDER

B ow in reverence
To the good and the difficult
To the soft and the harsh
Bow down with deep acceptance
To the light and the dark

This is the secret of surrender
A return to Oneness

That which I have seen, I cannot describe
That which I have experienced, I cannot express
I can only live the footprint of the experience

If my experience can be an example
For those who seek the good
Or if it will be mocked by fools
Is not in my control
There is no use in trying to control
I cannot catch the wind
But I can feel it
Be open to the spirit of the good
It surrounds you

Touched by infinity
Merging into the eternal
Through Divine silence
In inner silence
I shall wait as a new bride
In deep humility

When the masks come off
What remains?
A human figure
A figure that reflects fragility and beauty
The fragility belongs to the humanness
The beauty belongs to the Divine

A long lasting misunderstanding
Comes to a boiling point
Between me and myself
Between myself and the Creator
How to deal with all the inner forces
That cause pain and suffering?

I must not run from them
But absorb them and let them pass through me
And allow myself to pass through them
A process of crystallization
Summoning them as one who belongs directly to God
To sit with them and discover
The true nature of their strength

UNITY AWAKENING

A conscious state of unity
Is the outcome of surrender
In which the "I am" dissolves
And all that remains is the silence of unity

When there is an openness to truth
The divided thought can only move aside
To make space for

Light

    Grace

        Love

And the immense power of Unity

Accepting the essence of myself
Is to accept the essence of life itself

＊＊＊

Once again longing to *BE*
To become the essence of being
To become that which has no form

The journey from matter to Spirit
From Spirit to matter

In Unity with the Divine
Unions being formed
Of touching
Of being touched

To the magic of essence
The magic of understanding

Of Breath
    Of Peace
        Of Love
    Of Now
Of Life

To the magic of ME
The magic of YOU
The magic of simplicity that dwells in all

SELF LOVE

K nowing yourself
Is to know the Divine in you
To know that love exists within you

Being attentive to your needs
Even the simplest ones
Will bring clarity and intimacy with yourself
Reject your needs, and you reject yourself
Reject yourself, and you will be rejected

Love yourself and those around you
And you will be loved in return
Love is contagious
It will kiss you back

Giving and receiving
Is giving and receiving to ourselves
Sometimes we need to nourish ourselves with food
Sometimes with compassion
Sometimes it is motivation and movement

Self love is giving to yourself as well
Even to those aspects of you which are not as complete
The divided parts within you

Take good care of yourself
And take care of the love you have for yourself and
others

⁂

The touch of totality
Guides us to feel the touch of personal wholeness

There is no high nor low
No more nor less
All is One Great Whole
That moves in perfection

⁂

Before knowing self love
We have lived in separation
In conflict with ourselves and our surroundings

If we forget the interconnectedness
Between all aspects of ourselves
We remain in inner struggle and division

Self love is the ability to accept *all* the colors within us
From a space beyond duality
The place where there is no separation
Between our different sides
From here, wholeness IS

Self acceptance is the bridge to self love

HARMONY

May I open once again
To the sensations of my body
Without contraction
Without control
With no attempt to dominate my pain

To feel as if I am floating on water
Relaxing all of my body
Softening into my soul
May the current of life carry me weightless
Free from the burden of pain
In harmonious flow

Without compassion
You cannot have heroism
Without love for humanity
You cannot have love for the Divine
If you do not flow
You will not reach harmony
Without humor
You can expand only *so much*

**The harmonious balance in nature
Is the harmonious balance in you**

Self judgment results in external judgment
Self rejection leads to external rejection
Inner happiness brings outer happiness
Self love is answered by outer love
In love, the Creator will be known

**Engaging with the infinite inside me
Is to touch the entire universe**

Mitra Politi

She who seeks universal peace
Shall create inner peace
Peace within her own home
Peace within the tribe

RELATIONSHIP

I n our humanity
We are all essentially the same
Remember that wherever you go

Leave a crack of not knowing in relating to others
A crack which is free from opinions and conclusions
Meet each one without fixed ideas or judgements
About who or what they are
The meeting will be fresh and authentic

Everything exists in the here and now
Relationships also require this quality
Be in relationship with no past
So you can truly see the real person in front of you
To notice the changes that happen within him
As well as the changes that happen in you

Love is possible
When two people communicate
From the center of their being
It is not only a resting place
But a place of movement
Of growth and combined work

Love is not simply two people
Who are in the same place
It is two people looking in the same direction

Sometimes it is important
To allow relationships to wither
In the withering itself there is great beauty
And deep compassion
Like a tree shedding its leaves
Painless, yet with deep gratitude for what has been

⌁

Beauty will be preserved for longer
If you do not try to own it
Allow it to be, and it shall grow
Try to own it, and it will fade
Allow it to enter you
And it will melt your heart
In love for the world and for everyone

⌁

INNER PEACE

L ove and peace
Are not for superficial use
But rather a practice of deep inquiry

⚭

Inner war, outer war
Inner peace, outer peace
All that is within is reflected without

Once this understanding penetrates
It changes our essence
On one hand, so much responsibility
On the other hand, so many choices

When peace dwells within me
So will there be peace around me
The test is in making an inner choice for peace
Time and time again

Whenever the conflict arises within us
Whenever war is at hand

In humility and grace
May we choose inner peace

Inner peace is an end to war and separation
Inner peace is the beginning of harmony and unity

CREATION

D o not be a beggar
And go Begging to the Creator
When in fact Creation is within you

Give yourself the time and space
To meet the Creator within you
In this meeting
You will birth the new in your life

She who sees her own depths of being with clear eyes
Sees the depths of the ocean of creation

**A movement into the depths of your creation
Is the movement of the entire universe**

The slightest of movements
Ignites the strongest shift in you

HERE AND NOW

Collect yourself into the center of your being
To the awareness of all that is here and now
Discover freedom
In the immediate experience of NOW
In your beingness

Redemption from all suffering is here and now
Suffering disappears
In the power of the present moment

Things as they are
Remain always in the present moment
Only the mind and its thoughts
Attempt to dwell in the past or future

How did the simplicity of the moment vanish?
Actually, it did not…
It was simply hidden for a moment
In the pain of thoughts running to the past

Simplicity floats back
It has always been there for you

Love for Creation

   Is a vital love

   That is here and now

RESURRECTION

A new song
A song of rejuvenation
Which is born of understanding
A new song of a new spirit
Giving thanks to the one who watches over me
Who guides me in such moments
Guarding me and directing my way

The desire to let go overcomes the desire to hold on
The desire to heal overcomes the desire to shut down
The desire to breakthrough overcomes the desire to escape
The desire for light overcomes the desire for darkness
This power within me enables me to take the leap

Resurrection came
In letting go of the fear and contraction
In **breathing** in this moment
In seeking the knowledge in **not knowing**

Within the pure essence of life itself
There is a resting place
Where I can relax
Where there is a divine support

In non-duality lies acceptance
Two opposites living together in peace
This is the dwelling place of the soul

The will to conquer, I have set aside
The desire to prove, I have cast out to sea
The desire to become, I have shed like an old skin
Inspiration, I have kept close to my heart
The song within me, I have infused into my bones
The joy within me, I have shared with others
My disappointment, I have shattered into pieces
The Divine within me, I have kissed every day

And so I climbed the ladder of love
In this manner
I revealed myself to the greatness of love
To the greatness of silence
To the greatness of Spirit

Return to trust
To be real and authentic
Willing to express the depths of things
And expose what is inside
Without fear or self judgement
Moving from an inner knowing
Rather than according to the opinions of others

All parts of identity
And all aspects of personality
Are parts of the whole

If I judge myself
If I deny myself love
I distance myself from the eternal and whole
If I deny the voice within me
Or reject any part of myself
I will never find peace
But only glimpses of temporary relief

There is no other choice
But to dive into the waters of love
In those waters I shall bathe and cleanse myself
All that I am, in all my shapes and forms

Yet, I cannot do it on my own
I cannot do it without the Divine
Without the presence of the whole
In all Her shapes
In all His colors

A true moment of understanding
Is when understanding
Echoes deeply into one's being
From that depth something grows -
An integrated way of being
A correct expression of understanding

Endless possibilities

   Endless love

    Endless light

Revival comes
As inspiration carries me on her wings
Inviting me to open up my heart
Without worry or fear

From the darkness of the contracted mind
I have opened up to receptivity
From the struggle of separation
Unity has emerged
In detaching from harsh criticism and distortion
The touch of innocence has been reborn

The poetry of being flows of its own accord
Effortlessly and without pain
It flows from an inner prophecy
A prophecy that fills and fertilizes itself from within
Inner poetry that springs into endless space
Once again I spread my wings
To rejoice in flight

FREEDOM

We are here to discover our strength
And inner beauty
And from that knowing to grow
To exit the inner prison
That we have adopted in order to survive
And expand towards the freedom
Which is beyond it all

Free from anxiety
Open and calm to the level of each cell
Open to the Beloved
Longing for the grace of silence

In that longing I shall find the light
And sing a song of freedom

Songs I never wrote now see the light of day
People I've never met, find freedom
And so my soul comes closer to the Creator

To the power of Creation
An old prayer of fulfillment is in my heart
A prayer for love and for unity
Let it guide my way
I shall meet it at its origin
As it sets me free

Mitra Politi

HAPPINESS

What is the origin of happiness
And where does it lead?
Happiness comes from choosing what IS
From accepting it and cooperating with it

Happiness cannot be captured by a rope
Nor can it be put in a box
It can only be perceived in deep understanding
Of the oneness within you

Happiness is a side-effect of living a healthy lifestyle

INNER SILENCE

In the depths of all living things
There is a current
A flow of deep silence

Meditation is the technique
Of listening to your being
And merging with **the deepest sound of your soul**
The sound of silence

When your being encounters its own truest self
It is a meeting with the Divine
You become one with the Infinite

᥅◈᥅

Clearing the way
From all distracting elements
Each element
believes it is none other then the whole itself

The wholeness that dwells within me
Now hidden from my heart
Where did it go?

The slightest movement towards consciousness
Can reveal the wholeness within me
A deep rest within the inner void
Can expose the whole
Which has never moved
Which has never disappeared
That can never cease

Allow your self to rest into your wholeness
It will reveal itself to you in all its glory
The gift of wholeness
The gift of inner silence
Contains within it all the treasures of Creation

❧

This is a song to the Infinite
To that ever-expanding space
The space which collapses all barriers
Which envelops us all
And reveals our joy

To the Infinite that exists in all
I bow deeply
Through inner and outer stillness
In the eternal stillness
I find relief

I am returning to myself by the road of inner silence
Without definitions or boundaries

Come home to yourself my son
Come home to yourself my sister
Return to the space of Creation within you

THE MYSTERY

Know you are supported by the mystery
Know its excitement for you
Know that the Divine loves you unconditionally

In chasing after the light
It eludes me
When I run towards it
It pulls further away
When I become still and open up
It flows through me
Becoming

My breath

My body

My being

Simple gratitude for the light of Creation

THE JOURNEY

With no map to guide me
I travel to that uncharted space within me
That truest place of essence
Of **Truth Itself** which is my guide
Directing my footsteps

**Learn to know that place within you
And you will know goodness wherever you are**

When the journey began
It was full of sparks
Full of light, hope and enchantment

But the road is long and ever changing
Along it, you will find many difficulties
Learn to always walk towards the light and liberation

Fear of separation
And longing for unity
Are part of the experience of life
They are polarities that create just the right tension
For healthy acceleration and growth

Make this journey in complete alertness
The responsibility for your inspiration
The responsibility to cultivate presence
To learn to rest into your own being

Is on YOU

Own the responsibility for your own freedom

When facing a world full of mystery
Which way does the wind blow?
The wind of illusion
Pulls you towards evermore stimulation and escape
The wind of the the Divine
Blows towards growth and expansion
Towards vast inner skies…
Time and time again

The path I have chosen to walk
Is not easy, nor is it hard
It is simply the path itself

The path is full of every color of the rainbow
It contains all that is
With challenges and vast spaces

The path remains the road to the light
The road home to the Divine

GRATITUDE

B e grateful to all that is around you
To all that you see
And all that sees you
To all that you meet
In every experience

Gratitude in its highest form
Must begin between me and myself

Giving thanks for who I am
Being grateful to that friend within me
To that which resides in the depth of my being
The Divine in me
That vibrates in infinite silence

SPIRIT

K nowing how to water the inner garden
Is the art of the spiritual artist
She who fertilizes the spirit
Is the artist who's fruits will ripen

In choosing to plant your garden
In choosing to nourish the Spirit
Act with totality
Connect to the Divine
To All That Is

◈

Solitude is essential
In the journey to Spirit

The Spirit that blows

The Spirit that fertilizes

The Spirit that heals

The One Great Spirit

He who wants to know the Great Spirit
Will have to get acquainted with his own spirit
With his authenticity
And the heights of his own divinity

She who seeks salvation in the other
Awaits a miracle
She who saves herself
Creates a miracle

In my inner garden
The morning dew caressed me
A beam of sunlight warmed me
The struggle of resistance melted
Becoming once more a drop of beauty
Reflecting all

TRUTH

In the presence of truth
The "I am" dissolves
The insignificance of my identity
Finds its true proportion
Between myself and Infinity

Each individual has his own truth
Yet there is only one absolute truth

The absolute truth
Is without any compromise
Piercing through all illusions

The absolute truth
leaves us naked
In front of the tremendous power of the Divine

I was busy with myself…
In a fraction of a moment
The absolute truth penetrated
Through a crack in my window
It swept away all my illusions
It swept away all my fears
All my hopes
My nightmares and my sweet dreams
It left me naked
In front of the Infinite

The meeting with the absolute truth
Reflects our infinity
The light of truth does not fade
It's flame forever burns

In absolute Truth
I found absolute silence
Absolute emptiness
From all that my "I am" is carrying

The purity that comes with truth
Is so strong and yet, so refined
It leaves me in awe
In front of the essence of life itself

May we all live to meet the absolute
May we all live to experience it
May we all live to BE it

UNIVERSAL LOVE

Self love is a bridge to Universal love
The Great Love beyond all shape and form
Be alert to its presence
And even the smallest sparks
That expose themselves to you
Will serve to make this love grow
Just like small seeds
That need the water of our attention

Love the Divine and you shall be loved in return
In love, this relationship will deepen and grow roots

⌒∞⌒

Love for the other is temporary
Universal love is eternal

⌒∞⌒

The message of Universal love:

Be strong my son, in your intention and in your presence
Implement tranquility within yourself
Allow your eyes to be open wide and aim true
Allow yourself to be revealed to you once again

Choose happiness and joy over sadness and misery
You are free – you have always been
Know and do that which benefits you
Allow this to be your guide
Remember to dance, to move and to flow

Breathe in existence
And allow existence to breath with you
Beauty is everywhere
See it and let it in

Do not sow guilt and you will not feel guilty
Do not sow judgment and you will feel neither small nor big
Do not reject and you will not be rejected
Love yourself
Strengthen the spirit by working the body
Not by denying it

Take care of the goodness in your life and within you
So you can meet the true and authentic
Within yourself and in the other

Remember to enjoy love itself while it is there
So it can blossom into Universal love

ACKNOWLEDGEMENTS

Special thanks to my beloved and book editor Jessica Begin for all the support, love and the unity.

Many thanks to Prasad Moss for the support in translation and to Noam Galili for helping me to transcribe the manuscript. Deep gratitude to my friends Foster Gamble, Panache Desai and Brandee Alessandra for their presence, unfaltering support and friendship in my life.

A special thank you to my dear friend and guide Kimberly Carter Gamble for the support and the inspiration to always aim for the highest.

Gratitude to my friend and fellow traveler Gerard Powell.

Thank you to Tyohar Castiel who opened the doors of my being to meditation and inner silence.

Thank you to Taita Juan Chindoy for the generous sharing and guidance in the ways of his ancient culture.

And finally, gratitude to my lovely daughter Munay Sol Politi.

ABOUT THE AUTHOR

Mitra Politi is the Spiritual Director for Rhythmia Life Enhancement Center in Costa Rica. He is an intuitive healer, certified Acupuncturist, and practitioner of indigenous Colombian healing under the guidance of Taita Juanito Chindoy.

Mitra offers transformational workshops, and private coaching for entrepreneurs and CEOs interested in bringing a spiritual and holistic focus to their work in the world.

For the last 20 years, Mitra has been living in Costa Rica in an ecological and spiritual community called PachaMama. For many he years he maintained an Acupuncture clinic and designed and taught numerous transformational programs within the PachaMama community and abroad.

In 2012, Mitra was invited by Taita Juanito, an indigenous Colombian healer from the Inga and Siona nations to deepen his understanding of and connection to their ancient wisdom and healing methods. He continues alongside of Taita Juanito to this day.

A generous friend and guide to many, Mitra brings clarity, intuition and humor to every endeavor.

Bring Mitra's words off the page!

Visit www.insights-thebook.com to delve deeper into the world of Insights and find resources to deepen your own experience with meditation and mindfulness:

Access free guided meditations led by Mitra.

Find out about his upcoming speaking events, spiritual retreats, healing work, and virtual gatherings.

Connect with Mitra on Social Media, where he shares unique insights and has conversations with other thought leaders.

Facebook: https://www.facebook.com/mitrapoliti

Instagram: https://www.instagram.com/mitrapoliti/